BABY SEAL

Published in Canada by Fitzhenry & Whiteside, 195 Allstate Parkway, Markham, Ontario L3R 4T8
Published in the United States by Fitzhenry & Whiteside, 311 Washington Street, Brighton Massachusetts 02135

10 9 8 7 6 5 4 3 2

National Library of Canada Cataloguing in Publication Data
Lang, Aubrey
Baby seal

(Nature babies)
ISBN 1-55041-685-5 (bound).--ISBN 1-55041-726-6 (pbk.)

1. Seals--Infancy--Juvenile literature. I. Lynch, Wayne
II. Title. III. Series: Lang, Aubrey. Nature babies.

QL737.P64L34 2002   j599.79'139   C2002-900337-7

U.S. Publisher Cataloging-in-Publication Data
Library of Congress Standards
Lang, Aubrey.
Baby seal / text by Aubrey Lang ; photography by Wayne Lynch. -- 1st ed.
[32] p. : col. photos. ; cm.   (Nature babies)
Summary: A baby harp seal is born on the frozen Arctic Ocean with only his vigilant mother to care for him.
As he grows, he begins to show a little curiosity about his world and learn of its perils.
ISBN 1-55041-685-5
ISBN 1-55041-726-6 (pbk)
1. Seals -- Juvenile literature. [1. Seals.] I. Lynch, Wayne, 1948- . II. Title. III. Series.
599.79   [E]   21   2002   AC CIP

Fitzhenry & Whiteside acknowledges with thanks the Canada Council for the Arts, and the Ontario Arts Council for their support of our publishing program. We acknowledge the financial support of the Government of Canada through the Book Publishing Industry Development Program (BPIDP) for our publishing activities.

ONTARIO ARTS COUNCIL
CONSEIL DES ARTS DE L'ONTARIO

Canada Council   Conseil des Arts
for the Arts   du Canada

Design by Wycliffe Smith
Printed in Hong Kong

BABY SEAL

Text by Aubrey Lang
Photography by Wayne Lynch

Fitzhenry & Whiteside

BEFORE YOU BEGIN

Dear Reader,

We love to watch and photograph wild animals. Often they make us laugh; sometimes they make us cry. We wrote this book to share with you some of the exciting stories in the life of a baby harp seal, which most people will never see. We prefer to photograph animals in nature, not in zoos. And we take care never to harm our animal subjects or to interfere with them in any way.

To find the seals, we flew in a helicopter over Canada's Arctic Ocean off the coast of Newfoundland. We crawled on the ice like mother seals so we wouldn't frighten the pups. Sometimes it was so cold that our camera froze.

— Aubrey Lang and Wayne Lynch

TABLE OF CONTENTS

It is late winter on the ice off the coast of arctic Canada. This is the home of the black and silver harp seal. For several months, the female harp seals have been busy gobbling up as much fish, shrimp, and sea lice as they can. They need to store up fat, because soon they will give birth.

The frozen ocean is bumpy and covered with snow.
Mother seals swim under the ice, searching for cracks
and holes through which they can climb onto the surface.

It's a cold, windy place to raise a baby. The icy seal nurs-
ery is far from land. Here the seals are safer from hungry
wolves and foxes. They are also safe from polar bears,
which usually hunt farther north.

Thousands of seal mothers have gathered together to raise their pups on the ice. Father seals take no part in this.

The birth of a harp seal is very fast; it's all over in less than a minute. After the pup is born, the mother spins around and sniffs her baby. It's very important for her to memorize the smell and sound of her new pup. Later, she will have to recognize her own baby in a crowd of hungry pups waiting for their mothers to feed them.

Seals rarely have more than one pup. Even though the mother is very fat, she could never supply enough milk to feed twins.

A newborn harp seal is called a yellowcoat. Its fur gets stained when the pup is inside its mother. After three or four days, the pup's straw-colored coat is bleached white by the arctic sun. The fluffy pup is now called a whitecoat.

Mother harp seals are very caring. In the first two days after birth, the mother and her pup are never apart. If a neighbor gets too close, the mother seal complains loudly. To scare the visitor off, she lifts up her head, fans her whiskers, and growls. If this doesn't work, the angry mother chases the neighbor over the ice like a high-speed caterpillar.

Every three or four hours, the seal pup gets hungry and cries like a human baby. Maa...maa...maa. The mother rolls onto her side and lets the baby suckle from the two nipples on her stomach. The mother's milk is full of fat, and thick like a warm milkshake. The pup grows very quickly on this creamy diet.

When it is born, a harp seal is scrawny. But after only a week of nursing, the baby has puffed up like a balloon, weighing twice as much as it did at birth. Now it looks like a furry, stuffed sausage with a black nose and whiskers stuck on one end.

When the pudgy pup gets thirsty, it eats snow.

When a seal pup isn't nursing, it's snoozing. Often a pup will find a spot where it isn't quite as windy and cold—behind a pile of ice or beside a mound of snow. Sometimes it sleeps in the same spot day after day. The heat from its body melts into an icy hollow, shaped like a cradle.

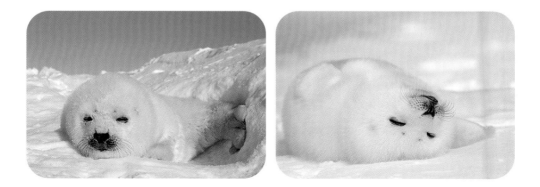

This female pup has an urge to wander. She's strong enough now to use her sharp front claws to wiggle and crawl over the ice and drifting snow. But the ice often cracks and splits into large pieces. A strong wind can shove the sections together and build a wall of broken ice that is too high and dangerous for a pup to cross.

Many harp seal mothers raise their young together on the same patch of ice, so pups have lots of young neighbors. Curious pups might approach each other or even sleep together. But the youngsters never play.

Some pups are grumps. When a neighbor comes to visit, the little one will bark. It might even slap the friendly visitor with a furry flipper.

One night there is a storm. The wind howls, the snow blows, and the ice groans. When morning comes, the blizzard has passed. The pups are covered with snow.

This female pup has kept warm through the night by the thick layer of fat under her skin. But now the pup is hungry, and she calls for her mother.

The pup doesn't know her mother has left for good. She is twelve days old now—the age when most harp seals are left on their own. The lonely pup cries for her mother over and over again, as she searches for her at the edge of the ice.

The ice is weak. It breaks, tossing her into the cold arctic water.

The pup is so fat that she floats like a cork. With her sharp claws she has no trouble pulling herself out of the water. It's not yet time for the baby harp seal to swim away. She will stay on the ice for another three weeks, living off her fat and molting her baby fur.

Like all seals, the young female has very big eyes. Her eyes will help her see when she hunts for her meal in the deep, dark water.

The harp seal has long whiskers, which will also help her catch food. Even when it is too dark for her to see, the young female's sensitive whiskers will feel the movement of the water when a fish swims by.

The young harp seal will be ready soon for life in the ocean.

DID YOU KNOW?

- There are nineteen different kinds of seals worldwide. Most of them live in the cold, rich waters of the Arctic and the Antarctic.

- Seals are closely related to walruses and sea lions. All of these mammals live in the sea and belong to the group of animals called pinnipeds, which means, "fin-footed."

- Adult female harp seals mate in March, soon after they abandon their pups. But the new baby seals don't start to grow inside the mother until early summer. This three- to four-month delay is common in many species of seals and sea lions.

- The mother harp seal does not eat during the 12 days she nurses her pup. She may lose 6 1/2 pounds (3 kg) of fat a day, eventually losing 1/4 of her total body weight. While the nursing mother is shrinking, her pup swells by 4 1/2 pounds a day (2 kg). In less than 2 weeks, the pup will triple its weight, going from 22 pounds (10 kg) to 74 pounds (34 kg).

- Harp seal mothers give birth at about the same time. Ninety-five percent of the mothers in an area will have their pups within a ten-day period around the first week of March.

- An adult harp seal may dive as deeply as 900 feet (274 meters), and stay underwater for more than 15 minutes.

- Small, schooling fish, such as capelin and arctic cod, are two of the favorite foods of the harp seal.

- In order to molt their old fur, adult seals must heat their skin by lying on top of the ice in the warm sunshine. It is only during this summer molting period that biologists can count the seals.

INDEX

BIOGRAPHIES

When Dr. Wayne Lynch met Aubrey Lang, he was an emergency doctor and she was a pediatric nurse. Five years after they were married, they left their jobs in medicine to work together as writers and wildlife photographers. For more than twenty years they have explored the great wilderness areas of the world — tropical rainforests, remote islands in the Arctic and Antarctic, deserts, mountains, and African grasslands.

Dr. Lynch is a popular guest lecturer and an award-winning science writer.

He is the author of more than a dozen titles for adults and children. He is also a Fellow of the internationally recognized Explorers Club, and an elected Fellow of the prestigious Arctic Institute of North America.

Ms. Lang is the author of nine nature books for children. She loves to share her wildlife experiences with young readers, and has more stories to tell in the Nature Baby Series.

The couple's impressive photo credits include thousands of images published in over two dozen countries.